Abraham

When Abram was seventy-five years old, he started out on a long, long journey. He didn't know where he was going. He didn't know how long the journey would take. But he went because God told him to, and Abram trusted God. He knew God wanted the best for him.

Abram didn't have any children when he
started the journey. He took with him Sarai,
his wife, and his nephew Lot. He also took all
his money, his sheep and goats and cattle,
and all his servants.

Before long, Abram had things to worry about.

First, there was not enough to eat, and many people were hungry. So Abram trekked into Egypt, where there was plenty of corn.

Abram and Lot bought all the food they
needed, but they didn't feel settled there.
They left Egypt and went into strange lands.

At last they came to a high hill overlooking a beautiful new country. Abram realized that he and Lot now had so many sheep and cattle that there would not be enough land for them all to graze upon.

"We'd better split up," Abram said to Lot. "You choose one way, and I'll go the other." Lot chose the land which was all green and grassy. It was the best land. Abram stayed where he was, in a land called Canaan.

Abram and Sarai were very sorry that they had no children. So Abram was very surprised when one night God told him that he would have many, many people in his family. God told Abram to look up into the night sky and count the stars. One day it would be just as hard to count all the people in Abram's family!

Abram was God's friend, and he often felt that God was speaking to him. It was years later when God made Abram the same promise again.

"Because you will be the father of a very special group of people," said God, "your name will be changed to Abraham."
Abraham meant father of many, many people.
God also told him to change his wife's name from Sarai to Sarah, which meant princess.

Abraham couldn't think how God's promise could come true. After all, he and Sarah were very old. They had seen a lot of sad things in their lives.

They had even seen whole cities destroyed because of the cruel things people had been doing to one another. But Abraham knew that God would keep his promise.

One hot day, when Abraham was sitting in the doorway of his tent, he was visited by three mysterious strangers. Abraham gave them something to eat and drink and waited to hear the reason for their visit.

He didn't have to wait long. They told Abraham that they would visit him in a year's time, when he would have a child of his own. Sarah burst out laughing. She just could not believe she would be a mother now!

But just when Abraham and Sarah thought all hope was gone, God amazed them both. A year later, Sarah had a baby. They called him Isaac, which meant laughter!

Abraham was thrilled. So was Sarah. God had kept his promise. Even though he was old, Abraham could see that through Isaac, and Isaac's children, and his children's children, he was going to be the father of many people.